THE BEL

CW00343335

THE BELL TOWER

POEMS BY
PAMELA CROWE

To any Bridgets out there

‽

THE EMMA PRESS

First published in the UK in 2022 by The Emma Press Ltd.
Poems © Pamela Crowe 2022.

All rights reserved.

The right of Pamela Crowe to be identified as the author of
this work has been asserted in accordance with the Copyright,
Designs and Patents Act 1988.

ISBN 978-1-912915-99-6

A CIP catalogue record of this book
is available from the British Library.

Cover design by Amy Louise Evans.

Printed and bound in the UK
by the Holodeck, Birmingham.

The Emma Press
theemmapress.com
hello@theemmapress.com
Birmingham, UK

Supported using public funding by
ARTS COUNCIL
ENGLAND
LOTTERY FUNDED

CONTENTS

150 WORDS AS I WAIT FOR A TREE TO GROW BACK

I (*or* anger)

Man at the back has cut down his tree
and now we are in a terrible romance
where each morning our eyes catch across the fence
before quickly turning away to focus on our tasks.

Man at the back is not tall enough for me
and fortunately married to his clever musician wife
(well done, man) and probably would not want me
with three kids and an anger problem.

Man at the back may just be stupid enough however
to like the idea of me, who probably looks
quite dazzling and blurred from over there
as anger doesn't travel well through windows and the kids
    are out of view.

Man at the back comes round to talk about the fence
that has blown over many times recently (since cutting
    down the tree)
and which he can't fix, him not being handy.
Man is stupid and looks intently at me.

SOCKS

I've returned to the haha
and sit with my back to the building.
The cattle are far off but will approach, I hope.
I build a plan for when they do.
To my left is my hand and to the right, my other.
My feet are socks filled with rice;
they knock heavy on the stones
and sometimes swing together, swing away.
Can you see me from the long window?
Hand by hand I lift grass and stones to pour
into the ditch. It takes years.
Over that time I have lost my children
and all the people who were near.
Some days I dribble soil, others I push
fingers into the wet ground and force
earth down to speed it up. I'm desperate.
Can you bring the children soon? I think.
But no one ever does. Some days I shout for them.
I scream and cleave.
Why won't someone bring them to me?
I make a pile of daisy heads and push them in one day.
A small stone follows them down.
'What's your plan?' I ask it.

Leaves blow and those I clasp I crush
with flat hands and cobbled rice.
I have lost the knowledge for standing because I forgot to try.
My legs look up at me so sad: 'How true is that,' they say.
'I'm throwing grass today, for pity's sake,' I say right back.
Eventually the cows approach. *At last*, I think.
I'm not ready – and puff up air to make
a hasty cloud they'll walk on. In dizziness and
clumsy I roll down and form the bridge
I sought to build.
The cows cross
and ratio the landscape.
You are all angry I have spoiled the view.

CLOUDCUNT

You, the cloud.

Oh look! there you are,

blobbing along as if you're best friends with rain

and thunder is your dad. Fuck off.

I don't need your fine spray, monthly deluge, spit.

Why not float the fuck off, oh ethereal beauty of porous pervicacity.

Oh heaven blocker, white witch carrier, look-of-lovely sugar spinner.

Arrows I shoot from my eyes to hasten your dispersal

and chants I stamp out to the sun man (who is another cunt)

to flirt his face into my skyline,

big enough to burn, you, off.

Fuck off, cloud.

INTO THE FIELDS

'To be of use' – Marge Piercy

Sad to be without the barrier of man, or ugly.

Or fucked.

Either way.

How helpful it was to be tucked away and rooted.

Marriage is an excellent fence and offers the girls a garden run with views to the lane

where the glad eyes stroll on Sundays browsing hedgerows

to fascinate the larkspur – or try to mow her.

Outside, and no longer a his,

she faulted to being an anyone's.

The cornflowers smoke from blue to blush

and now I have a crackle glaze they like

and too much cheek for me to live and gently bleed as I have loved.

New, childless, hunted, what use is this corporeal clam. Am I only man's?

Take hope I'll scathe you clear; my view needs courage and that's rare.

5

LENGTH

Go and be happy with someone else.
Not me.
Go and do twee things with her.
I am that drawer my dad had.
Heavy and hard to pull out
in the morning room, in the corner, where the light hits.

I'm full of sharp things, matches, opened packs,
soft cardboard, nails of different sizes, big long ones,
and a tiny lamp, the type that cookers need.

A drawer of meticulous, insistent ways of measuring air and
    force and length.

I'm half stuck open, at an angle and abandoned,
contents tipped forwards and towards.
There's a blade with cardboard on to save you,
and wall plugs the colour of tongue,
a hammer that's too heavy for most to lift
and a ruler bent double, hinges gold and scuffed.
It becomes a metre when it's opened and the world expands
    with it.

150 WORDS AS I WAIT FOR A TREE TO GROW BACK

II (*or* patience)

Woman at the back, one along, has cut down her tree
and now the infirm fence is even more fucked.
What is it with everyone undermining my fence
which was happily doing its job until recently?

Woman at the back tells me we should all get together
and work out a plan to sort out the fence
but I can't help feeling this is *something else*
coming from people who destroy perfectly good trees.

Woman at the back talks too much
and it is hard to end the conversation about my fence.
I would rather have a fence than have a talk
and I am grieving the fence that meant I didn't have to.

Woman at the back has been speaking to man at the back
and his wife and they are all in agreement.
I find the number for Richard who maintains boundaries
and though it is Saturday I call him.

CAT STRETCH

I've let the house go to shit
so I can get something meaningful done.
Come and see my dismal house.
Lonely from its things I thought would make us happy.

Now they all sit staring like the cats
asking me *What's next?*
I don't know. I'm listening to Lata Mangeshkar
and pretending I am fine.

In other news I'm writing lots
and stretching in the morning.
On the mat I keep a low profile
so as not to see the crap.

Co-minting

We're driving and I offer you a mint.
'I've gone double,' I say.
'Do you want to go double?'
'Yes please,' you say and *seem* pleased when I hand you two.
We sit adjacent sucking them in sync.
The time it takes is double too.
A brief reprieve from yelling
at you all.

LOVE LETTER HALLOUMI

Months go by for the feta and halloumi,
Not loved enough to eat or fry,
Wanted, just not enough.
Bought, but fridge-door sidelined.
Bypassed. Why?

This is me with you.
I keep you in the door on hold.
A year will pass and still not eaten,
Though the salted butter flies.
Flanked by ginger and a mummied garlic,
A pair of top shelf bookends. Uppity, spiteful, dry.

SEA

Sea drags me out. No, not sea, you.
Voluble force back and forth;
you don't even know
you're doing it.

Each time, arms stretched,
legs coathangered, I stick man
to the shore,
land gasping, lungs to fill;
I stand still looking back,
so inland, more inland this time.
You cannot get me now.

Drying, that takes weeks.
Wind ribbons to my face
and lifts my greening hair; on safe skin a dress
that buffers, tip-taps my tapered frame. I Flag.

It's warm though
and the breeze is fine by me, this sexless wind
that doesn't want me – just strides out my seaborne stare
and carols round like flossing saline
till you come in once more.

Stirring

Typing *thought provoking synonym* into laptop
for my new job at the Arts Council who must assume
I have prior mastery of new good words for old
words or they would not have employed me.

Typed *objective* and found *aim*, which will do, and
typed *secularism* but can't tell you why and
that's a word that no-one seems to want to talk about
apart from those confusing it with *speculum*.

Typed *stirring* into thesaurus and got *dramatic*,
which it was, but worried, concerned and fretful
by lack of words for *stirring* and *anxious* that
all language fails and there's nothing new, or rousing.

150 WORDS AS I WAIT FOR A TREE TO GROW BACK

III (*or* courage)

Woman at the back needs to pull down her blind
and seriously rethink where she sits getting dressed
as each morning I see her from afar
with hair dryer blasting sat totally fucking clueless in her bra.

Woman at the back is too tall and too fierce for me
and fortunately married to that rock climber chap
(git) and probably would not want me
with short legs and smalltalk anxiety.

Woman at the back might just be interested enough however
to like the idea of me who probably looks
quite forceful and decisive from over there
since self-doubt doesn't travel well through windows and my
wife is out of view.

Woman at the back suggests I try and fix the fence
that has blown over many times recently (since storms blew
down the tree)
and which her man can't fix, so I go round to see.
Woman is not interested and stares angrily at me.

Helen from Reprographics

Many Helens.
But only one in Reprographics.
One so able, so prompt.
So prudent and useful
within Reprographics. Excellent at
Facsimile, Xerox and Hole Punch.
Our thanks to Helen in Reprographics.

But Can You Believe Her?
Can You Forgive Her?
Helen from Reprographics.
Helen who hides in Reprographics.
Liar Helen.
Helen the Liar.
The Reprographic Liar called Helen.

Envious of Helen from Reprographics
who can just reproduce graphics
from behind a door with Reprographics written on it
when we are so concerned.
Helen who won't let us help her.
Helen who won't tell us where she's going this summer
or who she loves.

ALL THE BOYS GO SOFT AND SAD

All the boys go soft and sad
when I am around.
Is it my delicious floorboards
or the pencil I keep dropping
on your wife's nose?
My fine eyes, good books, metal tin of askance looks,
obedience, and prettyish little kind of wilderness?

Is it how you look at me
when I turn away?
Ungiving neck on sweet neat face
with no mouth to square to you.
She's a quiet one.

All the boys go soft and sad
when I turn the stairs
in separated daylight to pick up my pencil.
Is it how my three bowls line up
hot, cold and half way towards you,
filled to disappointment
with no new normal?

Chiroptera

The sky is a thousand black umbrellas,
really,
a thousand black umbrellas,
all open and aghasting side by side.
Every miscreant and friend has opened one
and I am sheltered by their confidence and alibis.

Sheltered I say,
but stopped and altered.
Lightlessness is dark, it is a gown.
And I am under, charcoaled, interrupted,
as far away each absence gathers ground.

'Stop. The damp is coming', choral voices.
'Secede your fear, sit still, you need not speak'.
They lie. My eyelid moves and hazels motive
to seize a thousand handles
J
    ust out of reach.

I summon
witches in black bonnets to delete them,
cast vehement draughts to maledict these paras wide.
But they don't come and I am left to understand that
the answer's just me, darling, standing, at full height.

Vertical, intended, mincing sonnets,
or lone at night in glass patagial baths,
you, me, Plathy, Woolf, Jane,
we're the tallest.
The darkness ours, worn highest, we are bats.

Fix

One tampon left, a super, and the last strong coffee in the house.

I worry when I place the problematic hygiene product on the bath edge

cliff top, chalky, above the precipice below.

Which is my bathroom floor in fact,

with coffee cup a brown low pool, sat ready for the flea trapeze to drop.

As if propelled by fear, mine, its,

the product rolls to death, an abject luge from the life it sees ahead and doesn't want.

Inserted, dark, soon spent and flushed

(yes, flushed).

While I, aghast, see both the coffee and the product rendered nothing in one foul

twin foil. Bitch.

I cannot be alert or bloodless now.

What day is this?

The tampon in the bin, I stuff my pants with paper and blind hope,

gaze down at the coffee, think

Is it safe?

Dave told me about this once, the 3x times rule when things go wrong.

Chant *It doesn't matter, matter, matter,*

even if it does.

I drink.

Ways in which I am Darcy

I am slow to trust.

I am busy thinking, not speaking.

I don't like dancing in front of people.

I have excessive pride.

It's hard to recover from challenges to it.

I'm open to changing.

I like high ceilings.

I like walking.

I like Derbyshire.

I like Elizabeth Bennet.

I like to burst into rooms and tell people I love them.

My good opinion once lost is lost forever.

150 WORDS AS I WAIT FOR A TREE TO GROW BACK

IV (*or* mercy)

Man at the back has stopped catching my eye
and now I'm in a terrible despair
where each morning I stand pressed up at the glass
trying hard to make him swivel in his ergonomic chair.

Man at the back keeps his head fixed at the screen
and won't so much look sideways to acknowledge me
(well done, man) and probably has decided I'm not dazzling after all
or I'm too old or too angry or too ugly or too tall.

Man at the back might just like the sight of me however
doing stretches (multitasking), hanging laundry in all weather
as I limber up and wobble, trying to propriecept this world
wondering who can want this tyrant cum heretic cum sad girl.

Man at the back comes down one day to monitor the fence
which has withstood a pandemic and my year as malcontent.
As my eye contact holds payload for the trees ripped from my land,
I say to him: *Plant saplings now.* He takes one from my hand.

WHAT IS IT?

I

We stood around it on the sand, five of us
poking sticks at it.
What is it? they asked.
It was red and filleted, soft, pink, prone,
placental,
and the dregs
of something having ebbed, now drowsy.
Is it a fish? he asked.
No. Not a fish, I said.
It's not moving, she said.
No, I said.
What is it though? he asked.
Their tiny sticks pushing and flicking.
Stop it.
Stop it, that's enough. Leave it, I said.
But it's dead.
No, I said. I don't think so.

II

I saw it, love's
vast attempt to live
past tolerance and pity,
past hope and what'll be.
They pulled drift and weed around it
to make it seem more dead
and ribboned off to play in cute directions
made sense only by the freezing wind.
I stood near to it collecting pebbles,
watching over till we had to leave.

JOHNSTONES

after Fleur Adcock

I have no excavations in my garden, only tombstones of the Johns.
Wonky heads of dead boys sit half-sunk across the lawn
and make the grass a job to cut.
I would have loved you in my way, had you shared and not told me to stop.

Why grow to angry men who didn't like it when
my sweet neat face met theirs at shoulder height or No.
The laundry dapples child-forms on their sadness and joys a line of T-shirt hope
and what can come from love, real love that likes my voice just as it is.

I'll bring you back, you'll gasp for air.
If you can start again, I'll press for start again.
I would have loved you in my way, I think, dodging shadows and your hazards,
pushing cornflowers through my hair.

Auto door

Two men spat at me in the Royal Park
and the landlord wouldn't throw them out
and looked so forlorn that I looked back in horror.
That was a mistake.
You can still smell it on me.
It's complicated.

It's ok.
The library stairs twist down to history and back up again.
I ripped out a page from Warhol with blue flowers on.
The buildings let you walk through them, if you know the route.
It's ok.

It's ok.
I can walk to the cinema in snow and back on my own.
It's ok.

I don't know who sent those boys
to the student bar in Newcastle
or why they kicked me to the ground.
Some bleak son of an angry man
from an island on the west no doubt –
revenge for my deserting Irish genes
or for not quite knowing who I was back then.
I go back to myself and lean my head on to my head
to tell her about love.

Lucy

What right to silence and inactivity do we have   Is the stripping of consciousness a
violent insist   To act or not act not my choice   Must we know what's on our mind
To live exposed when we chose   To confuse ourselves   Ignore one call out of our
voice and hear another   What women have we written of that did not know their mind
And so we wrote another for them   Perhaps we did not ask   Or preferring not their choices
Chose another for them   Could I write four chapters of how you don't know yours   And
get dug in to gouge the meaning from you   And call you by that after, you being fixed.
Assuming we're unknowable and every person here another us   Why not write that
writing is not knowing what the ending is.

CHRISTMAS COPE

or The Clementine

I'm writing to commend our dearest Wendy.
It's 1 a.m. and I am on the loo.
I'm reading *Family Values* while I contemplate
what Christmas means to her to me to you.

She's older now, she must be, as I know
I am. Her sentences run over like
the wine. She's direct, warm, inventive and so citrus
-y; her words a gift, my Christmas clementine.

ACKNOWLEDGEMENTS

'What is it?' on page 22 was first published in The Poetry Society's *Poetry News*.

NOTES

The Bell Tower is a book of love poems; love in all its forms. It's also a book about fear, threat, and estrangement. I wanted to assert a space where I could write freely, with courage and without risk. I imagined myself at the top of a campanile (bell tower) in the remote mountain village of Carbini, Corsica, a place I visited after reading Dorothy Carrington's *Granite Island*. The campanile is a space of my own with a great view from which to shout across the landscape. This book is The Bell Tower.

Thanks to Jane Austen and Helen Fielding for writing books I can never get enough of and for creating characters who liberated me to laugh at myself, to stop seeking approval and to hold out for respect. Thanks to Wendy Cope and John Donne for showing how poetry can be a site of intense joy, desire, and loss. Thanks to my dear friends, I'm indebted to your constancy and I love you. Thanks to my children, who I love beyond words.

ABOUT THE POET

Pamela Crowe is an artist and writer based in Leeds. Her practice focuses on words and how we say them, on text, voice and performance. Her work has been shortlisted for the 2019 Bridport Poetry Prize, longlisted in the 2020 National Poetry Competition, and published in The Poetry Society's *Poetry News*. *The Bell Tower* is her first book.

ABOUT THE EMMA PRESS

The Emma Press is an independent publishing house based in the Jewellery Quarter, Birmingham, UK. It was founded in 2012 by Emma Dai'an Wright, and specialises in poetry, short fiction and children's books.

The Emma Press has been shortlisted for the Michael Marks Award for Poetry Pamphlet Publishers in 2014, 2015, 2016, 2018, and 2020, winning in 2016.

In 2020 The Emma Press received funding from Arts Council England's Elevate programme, developed to enhance the diversity of the arts and cultural sector by strengthening the resilience of diverse-led organisations.

Website: theemmapress.com
Facebook, Twitter and Instagram:
@TheEmmaPress